DATE		
APR 2 0 1999			
		SEP 1 5 2000	
MAY 1 2 1999			
JUL 2 7 1999			
SEP 2 6 1999			
AUG 0 2 2000			

DOGS SET II

Beagles

Stuart A. Kallen
ABDO & Daughters

visit us at
www.abdopub.com

Published by Abdo & Daughters, 4940 Viking Drive, Suite 622, Edina, Minnesota 55435.

Printed in the United States.

Cover Photo credits: Peter Arnold, Inc.
Interior Photo credits: Peter Arnold, Inc.

Edited by Bob Italia

Library of Congress Cataloging-in-Publication Data

Kallen, Stuart A., 1955-
    Beagles / Stuart Kallen.
    p. cm. -- (Dogs. Set II)
    Includes index.
    Summary: An introduction to the smallest member of the hound family, which includes its history, development, uses, and care.
    ISBN 1-56239-572-6
    1. Beagles (Dogs)--Juvenile literature. [1. Beagles (Dogs) 2. Dogs.] I. Title. II. Series: Kallen, Stuart A., 1955- Dogs. Set II.
    SF429.B3K35   1998
    636.753'7--dc21

                                        97-15715
                                        CIP
                                        AC

Contents

Dogs and Wolves—
Close Cousins

Dogs have been living with humans for more than 12,000 years. Today, millions of dogs live in the world. Over 400 **breeds** exist. And, believe it or not, all dogs are related to the wolf. Some dogs—like tiny poodles or Great Danes—may look nothing like wolves. But under their skin, every dog shares many feelings and **traits** with the wolves.

The dog family is called Canidae, from the Latin word *canis*, meaning "dog." The canid family has 37 **species**. They include foxes, jackals, wild dogs, and wolves.

Opposite page: Beagles huddled together under a log.

Beagles

Beagles are called "merry little hounds with big hearts."

Beagle is a French word meaning small. The dogs were used over 400 years ago to hunt rabbits and pheasants. Paintings from the 1600s, 1700s, and 1800s, show beagles hunting. Beagles were brought to the hunting fields in the pockets of hunting coats.

Over time, people selected larger beagles to **breed** and their size grew. Beagles got their hunting **traits** from miniature bloodhounds, foxhounds, and coonhounds. Beagles were brought to America in the 1860s.

Opposite page: Beagles are good hunters.

What They're Like

Beagles are hounds who use their noses to hunt. They are friendly and get along well with other pets. They are smart and love children. They are brave. Beagles are always ready to run. Their excitement and joy can be heard in their bark. They do like to howl, which might be a problem if they are kept in a city.

Beagles love to be outdoors. They do not mind bad weather or wild hillsides. Hunters prize beagles because of their ability to hunt cottontail rabbit, squirrel, and pheasant.

Opposite page: Beagles are friendly dogs.

Coat and Color

A beagle's **coat** is a close, hard, hound coat of medium length. Beagles may be black, brown, or white.

Beagles have short, hard hair.

Beagles have white, brown, and black hair.

Size

There are two varieties of beagles. Those who measure 13 inches (33 cm) or under, and those who measure 13 to 15 inches (33 cm to 38 cm) in height. These heights are measured at the shoulder. Adult beagles under 13 inches (33 cm) weigh about 18 pounds (8 kg). Dogs over 13 inches (33 cm) weigh about 20 pounds (9 kg).

Beagles have long, wide ears, soft brown or hazel eyes, and a straight, square jaw.

Opposite page: These beagle puppies are playing with each other.

Care

Beagles make happy members of any family. They are people-pleasers.

Like any dog, a beagle needs the same thing a human needs: a warm bed, food, water, exercise, and lots of love.

Beagles have short hair that needs to be brushed once a week. Sometimes the dog will need a bath and its nails clipped. All dogs need shots every year. These shots stop diseases such as **distemper** and **hepatitis**.

As a member of your household, your dog expects love and attention. Beagles enjoy human contact and like to play fetch. They love to run and explore.

Beagles love human contact.

Feeding

Like all dogs, beagles like to eat meat. But beagles need well-balanced diets. Most dog foods—dry or canned—will give the dog proper **nutrition**.

When you buy a puppy find out what it has been eating and continue that diet. A small puppy needs four or five small meals a day. By six months, it will need only two meals a day. By one year, a single evening feeding will be enough.

Beagles must be exercised every day so they do not gain weight. Walking, running, and playing together will keep you and your dog happy and healthy. Give your dog a hard rubber ball to play with.

Like all animals, beagles need fresh water. Keep water next to the dog's food bowl and change it daily.

Like all dogs, beagles need a well-balanced diet.

Things They Need

A dog needs a quiet place to sleep. A soft dog bed in a quiet corner is the best place for a beagle to sleep. Beagles should live indoors. If the dog must live outside, give it a dry, **insulated** dog house.

Beagles love to play and explore. A fenced-in yard is the perfect home for the dog. If that is not possible, use a chain on a runner.

In most cities and towns, dogs must be leashed when going for a walk. A dog also needs a license. A dog license has the owner's name, address, and telephone number on it. If the dog runs away, the owner can be called.

Opposite page: A beagle on a leash.

Puppies

An average beagle can have up to six puppies. The dog is **pregnant** for about nine weeks. When she is ready to give birth, she prefers a dark place away from noises. If your dog is pregnant, give her a strong box lined with an old blanket. She will have her puppies there.

Puppies are tiny and helpless when born. They arrive about a half hour apart. The mother licks them to get rid of the birth sacs and to help them start breathing. Their eyes are shut, making them blind for their first nine days. They are also deaf for about ten days.

Dogs are **mammals**. This means they drink milk from their mother.

After about four weeks, puppies begin to grow teeth. Separate them from their mother and give the puppies soft dog food.

A beagle puppy just a few weeks old.

Glossary

breed: a grouping of animals with the same traits.

coat: the dog's outer covering of hair.

distemper: a contagious disease that dogs and other animals get, which is caused by a virus.

hepatitis (hep-uh-TIE-tis): an inflammation of the liver caused by a virus.

insulation (in-suh-LAY-shun): something that stops heat loss.

mammal: a group of animals, including humans, that have hair and feed their young milk.

nutrition (new-TRISH-un): food; nourishment.

pregnant: with one or more babies growing inside the body.

species (SPEE-sees): a kind or type.

trait: a feature of an animal.

veterinarian: a doctor trained to take care of animals.

Internet Sites

Twainheart Beagles
http://www.teleport.com/~canderso/
Cute puppy pictures and information for Beagle lovers and people considering adding a Beagle to their family. General information, breeding information, how to choose a beagle, and much more on this site.

The American Kennel Club Online
http://www.akc.org/
The American Kennel Club can help you begin your research with its pictures and descriptions of each breed recognized by the AKC. Your initial research will help you narrow the field when it comes to selecting the breed for you and your lifestyle. Remember to consider your dog's lifestyle, too. And for extended research, consult the resources at your local library.

Beagles on the 'Net
http://www.simcom.on.ca/~sfrost/
Hi. Welcome to The Ultimate Beagle Home Page. This Page Includes Pictures of my Beagle Griffey, A Downloadable Movie, Beagle Links, and Cute Animated Pictures. Enjoy!

These sites are subject to change. Go to your favorite search engine and type in Beagles for more sites.

Index